A Desert Place

Adolfo Quezada

Illustrated by Robert Manning

LIVING FLAME PRESS
BOX 74 LOCUST VALLEY, N.Y. 11560

Cover: Robert Manning

All scripture quotations are from the *Jerusalem Bible*

Copyright 1982: Adolfo Quezada

ISBN: 0-914544-40-3

Published by: Living Flame Press/Box 74/Locust Valley, N.Y. 11560

Printed in the United States of America

*Lovingly dedicated
to my parents.*

Acknowledgements

Thank you to my wife, Judy, who offers so much of herself to me. Her inspiration and support helped me write this book.

Thank you to those who have believed in me and have had the patience and generosity to read this material and offer honest feedback: Pat Roads and Sister Anne Burns.

Thank you to the many authors of the books which have helped me to grow in spirit through the years. May this book repay some of that indebtedness.

This book is a prayer. Its words are few, its message simple and direct. Read it with your heart, as well as your mind, and allow your soul to search its source, he who calls you to a desert place.

Introduction

The pages you are about to read are the revelation of a man's soul. The man is Adolfo Quezada.

Adolfo would not want me to say very much about him. He will not even know what I write before the publisher receives this. I share with you the following, because I believe it will be helpful to know something about this man who is going to reveal himself to you.

I have known Adolfo for the past ten years. I have been his pastor, his friend and his co-worker. Adolfo is a husband and father, an administrator at the University of Arizona, and a friend to many.

He is thoroughly involved with real life, with real people, and with all the real stuff that comes with such involvement. It is important to me, at least, to know this about a person who writes to me about prayer.

Adolfo is concerned about human joy and pain, about human rights and justice and growth. At St. Pius X Parish in Tucson he conceived and brought to maturity a program called "Hermanos" (Spanish for "Brothers and Sisters"). Hermanos is a unique, non-paternalistic process of matching and befriending families from different ethnic, cultural and socio-economic backgrounds. He also authored a service known as "Nosotros" (Spanish for "Us"), a referral and advocacy agency which is funded by the Tucson United Way.

I tell you these things because you are about to look into the soul of Adolfo Quezada. The pages which follow are about prayer, about his struggle to come to deeper union with God. His struggle is the struggle of the ordinary person who takes God seriously.

Sometimes these pages may appear to be mystical, and they are. But this will not disturb us when we realize that all of us ordinary folk are called to a mystical experience of God. Probably most of us have already had such experience, but have hesitated to name it because we feel that mysticism is for someone holier than we.

This short book will be encouragement to us ordinary folk who struggle with prayer, and wrestle with God. It is encouraging because it comes from the core of a man such as we — a man, whose prayer has immersed him deeply into the reality of life and of people.

I am grateful to Adolfo for sharing himself in these pages.

— Rev. Msgr. Robert D. Fuller
National Office of RENEW
Newark, New Jersey
January 10, 1982

Preface

I offer this book to you as a part of myself. Parts of it were written as private prayer, not intended for public view. It became clear to me, however, that I could not write a book about prayer without sharing the essence of what prayer has been to me. Consequently, I included some of my most intimate thoughts and feelings which have been my prayers.

Jesus is the thread which is woven through the book. It was, after all, this man who pointed us to an intimate unity with God as the purpose of life, and to prayer as the means to that communion.

A *Desert Place* was written by a man in search of his basic self. Hopefully, its ministry will be among those who have become serious about their own awakening spirituality. It offers a response to the need for the quiet care of the soul.

The book speaks of life and communion with God. This communion, which is prayer, grows only where the soil has been prepared. Before prayer can begin the heart must be free of chains that bind.

Scripture and experience tell us that prayer must be free from expectations that limit and deform. When we place God out of reach or when we stereotype him by our concepts, our prayers are frustrated before they begin.

We must also remember that sanctity does not produce prayer, but rather, prayer evolves into sanctity. Prayer takes the form of life and life takes the form of the moment at hand.

This book was not written to teach anyone how to pray, for prayer is the natural expression of our love for God and the reflection of his love for us.

In scripture we find that Jesus was especially dependent on his Father. He found he had to return constantly to quiet solitude in order to live the life he was called to live. We too are called to solitude and rest.

The love of God means our presence to him. All we are and all we do must revolve around the hub of prayer.

Prayer is an integration of body, mind and spirit. It is a constant struggle to remain conscious of God's presence, and a constant dismissal of distracting preoccupations.

Our prayer becomes a quiet listening of the soul. Our silence invites his presence and the world he gives us comes alive. It is through prayer that we let God live through us but first, we must surrender the illusions we have about ourselves and the world.

True prayer is honest and sincere, but it is also a risky business because we are called to answer God's prayers in us.

Our spirit turns to life and love, and love for God is love applied. Prayer brings us to the fullness of our humanity. It seeks not our will but that of God. The only real need we have is for communion with our Father.

Through prayer, the Father calls us to love him intensely and completely. He calls us, not to goodness, but to fullness; not to righteousness, but to consciousness. The cost of this consciousness is all that we have and more. It is a consciousness, not of peace, not of heaven, not even of love, but of him alone.

A *Desert Place* reveals the darker side of the spiritual path. You will be able to share the joy of oneness with God, but you will also identify with the dark nights of faithlessness, and with the constant struggle between the soul and the world.

When we feel most abandoned, God is most present to us. Our heart knows no greater pain than that of separation, and yet it is not he who leaves us. It is we who flee from him.

From the ashes of faithlessness comes the spark of the Love that saves us. Agony of absence turns to ecstasy of union, but only for a season.

Contents

Contents

I

A Desert Place

"And rising up long before daybreak, he went out and departed into a desert place, and there he prayed."[1]

There, in the midst of darkness and the quiet of his soul, death came to Jesus and the Christ was born. Love was his milk, communion was his meat and the life of Christ was the prayer of God.

Can it be, dearest Father, that this intimate union with you is the paramount purpose of my existence? For this I was born: that I might return to the house of my Father, there to remain forever more.

Jesus believed man's truest nature is to " . . . love the Lord your God with all your Heart, with all your soul, and with all your mind."[2] He knew that the inevitable conse-

quence of such a love is to "... love your neighbor as yourself."[3]

But how do I come to love with this completeness, this surrender? For Jesus it was through prayer, as it is for me also.

It is in my heart, in the depths of my being, that my soul begins to pray, for that is its deepest impulse. It is by instinct that I seek my source, for only through prayer can I remember that my nature is God-like.

I am. I have always been and I will always be. My physical being is vulnerable, but my spirit is part of the Invincible Soul.

When I look into your face, Father, I see the reflection of my own true self. When I give myself to you in prayer, you come to life within me. I change from who I want to be to whom you are in me. Your love meets mine and conceives the kingdom of heaven in my heart, as your Son was conceived in the womb of Mary.

"... but the angel said to her, 'Mary, do not be afraid; you have won God's favor. Listen! You are to conceive and bear a son, and you must name him Jesus.'"[4]

And Jesus was born of Mary, as he is born of those who love you in prayer.

Prayer is the umbilical cord that gives life from the Mother God. It is the river that

returns to the sea. More basic than food for
my body is prayer for my soul.

II

The Soil Must Be Prepared

Prayer is not magic nor a step beyond the real. It is like a tree planted in the soil of life which grows as it is pruned. But first, the soil must be prepared.

A voice in the desert crying out, "Make a straight way for the Lord," [5] reminds me to clear the path for the God who comes in love. More important than any form of meditation is that my heart be free of the chains that bind.

"So then, if you are bringing your offering to the altar and there remember that your brother has something against you, leave your offering there before the altar, go and be reconciled with your brother first, and then come back and present your offering."[6]

How often I attempt to pray with malice

23

in my heart. I turn to you, dear Father, resenting the offences of my brother, condemning the ways of others, expecting the worst from life or ignoring the debts I have incurred.

Help me to forgive my brother, to cease my judgment, and to nurture hope in what can be. Help me to believe that:

For the pain I caused today, you have forgiven me.

For the ways of love I have not travelled, you have forgiven me.

For the child in me I have turned away, you have forgiven me.

For putting other gods before you, you have forgiven me.

For plans and schemes of independence, you have forgiven me.

For times of panic and despair, you have forgiven me.

For fears about all my tomorrows, you have forgiven me.

For not appreciating your gift of moment, you have forgiven me.

For wasting talents and hiding tools, you have forgiven me.

For holding on to what must die, you have forgiven me.

For not forgiving, you have forgiven me.

The chains that bind are also of another nature. My prayer is preceded by a myriad of expectations about the course that should be travelled and the landmarks to be found. Help me, Father, to break these chains that I may come to know you as you are, and not as I would have you be.

III

Expect the Unexpected

To dare to pray is to plunge into the waters of the unexpected.

For many years the Jews expected a Messiah to come to deliver their people. When Jesus made himself known to them, however, they rejected him as the Christ because he did not meet their expectations of a "deliverer."

"In him was life, and the life was the light of men. And the light shines in darkness; and the darkness grasped it not."[7]

In the same way, I fail to recognize you in prayer, Father, because of my expectations of who, what, where, and why you are.

I must erase the images I have of you; forget the thoughts and concepts I hold of you; approach you with an open mind, an open heart and soul.

I must not confine you to a theory or philosophy. Rather, I must let you make yourself known to me as you will.

"The wind blows wherever it pleases; you hear its sound, but you cannot tell where it comes from or where it is going. That is how it is with all who are born of the Spirit."[8]

Even Peter had his own expectations of the nature of God.

As Jesus knelt to wash his feet, Peter rejected the gesture as beneath the person of Jesus. Peter was to learn that the love of God has no limit, and is reflected at all levels and in many ways.

As I pray to you, dear Father, let me consider the vastness of your being.

❖━━❖

Not O joyous wonder, but O little child's face.

Not O Lord of Lords and Host of Hosts, but O the twinkle in the old man's eye, O redness of the flower.

Not O God of all creation, but O Lover of infinitesimal me.

❖━━❖

When I am disappointed in my prayer life, what is unfulfilled is not my prayer, but my expectations.

Is it an answer to a question that I seek through "inspiration"? For this, I would have much better luck inquiring of a computer. Is it a shopping list of needs I submit to the Father? Perhaps I should ask a genie. Is it a fearful, guilt-filled compulsion to acquiesce? If so, I may have made God into a tyrant.

Let go. Let *him* be.

Sometimes we think prayer is extremely difficult, and that it is reserved for the wise and saintly. "I'm just an ordinary person," we say. "What do I know about talking with God, much less hearing him?"

But can it be that this awareness of our littleness is what enables us to enter through the narrow gate of prayer? Is this what Jesus meant when he prayed:

"I bless you, Father, Lord of heaven and of earth, for hiding these things from the learned and the clever and revealing them to mere children. Yes, Father, for that is what it pleased you to do."[9]

When we depend on the power of our intelligence and discernment alone, we become frustrated at our blindness or defeated by our inability to comprehend. It is only through

28

humble faith in the grace of God that we can come to understand the nature of his kingdom.

" ' . . . unless a man is born from above, . . . he cannot see the kingdom of God.' "[10]

Sometimes we think that prayer is a mood created by external conditions, that without certain rituals or sacred places and practices there can be no prayer. But prayer is not the formal religious performance that it is sometimes made out to be.

Prayer is not synonymous with religiosity. Often we are taken up with the organizational aspects of our churches and the transactions attached to their maintenance. We become too preoccupied with the rules, regulations, customs and traditions of religion. We need to be reminded almost daily of the words of Jesus to the legalists of his day:

"Alas for you, scribes and Pharisees, you hypocrites! You who clean the outside of cup and dish and leave the inside full of extortion and intemperance. Blind Pharisee! Clean the inside of cup and dish first so that the outside may be clean as well."[11]

At times, I feel my heart on fire with your presence, Father, but prayer is not only ecstasy atop a mountain.

In the dark periods of my life I look for you to ease the pain, to soothe my wounds, to help me understand, for prayer is sometimes a valley.

The drought that comes my way leaves me barren, lonely, searching for the Light, for prayer is sometimes a desert.

In daily living there is little romance. The routine of labor, the heavy anchor of responsibility and the personal conflicts which arise can dull the mind and spirit, but through it all we must remember that prayer is sometimes found in the marketplace.

Prayer is seeing the world in all its glory. Prayer is not seeing, yet believing, in the presence of the Spirit.

Prayer is expecting the unexpected.

IV

A Force Through Which to Live

"Lord, teach us to pray..."[12] asked a man of the Master. But no lessons ensued, no techniques were imparted. Prayer, to Jesus, was not a form but a force through which to live.

In the words that he gave to his disciples was the spirit of prayer itself:

"Our Father in heaven, may your name be held holy, your kingdom come, your will be done, on earth as in heaven. Give us today our daily bread. And forgive us our debts, as we have forgiven those who are in debt to us. And do not put us to the test, but save us from the evil one."[13]

The words of Jesus were gentle, but direct. His plea was selfless, but demanding. His prayer announced the nearness of our Father,

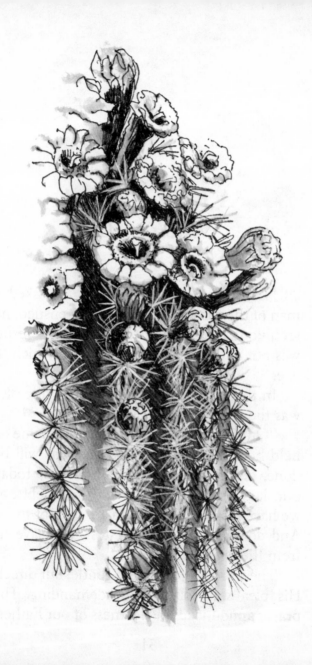

even in our hearts. It proclaimed the coming of the kingdom of heaven as our wills dissolve in his. It declared our interdependence with the one true Source as his love becomes our bread.

This was all that Jesus would say, for he knew the seed of prayer had been planted in the heart of man. He knew there are as many ways to pray as there are ways to say, "I love you." And he knew that each of us must find the way which serves us best at each moment of our lives.

What is essential is that our prayer include all that we are at the moment. It may arise out of spiritual affluence or out of next to nothing. Neither the length nor the form of our prayer is as important to God as its authenticity.

Our prayer is not unlike the two copper coins offered to the treasury by the poor widow. They did not compare to the sizeable amounts contributed by the wealthy, but in Jesus' eyes she had given more than all the others. " . . . for they have all put in money they had over, but she from the little she had has put in everything she possessed, all she had to live on."[14]

I may not pray today, Dear One, but I will hear the morning sparrows.

I may not even speak to you, but I will greet the total stranger.

I may not feel you in my heart, but others' love will fill my cup.

I may not think of you today, but I will be present to my brother.

I may not seem to be with you, but I will know you are with me.

———❖———

My prayer may come from gratitude or may be inspired by my love for you, Father. I may want to confess, to sing out with joy, or just to be in communion with you.

I can pray on my knees, on my back or sitting. I can walk with you in the desert or meet you in the chapel. I can hear you in music or in the bustle of the city. I can share with you my laughter or my crying or my silence.

Like the flowers of Spring that give birth to a season, my prayers begin your reign. It matters not to my King if they are roses or daisies, but that their root is love and their color, your truth.

V

A Call to Rest

Jesus grew in fame " . . . and large crowds would gather to hear him and to have their sickness cured, but he would always go off to some place where he could be alone and pray."[15]

But if his ministry was to spread the gospel and to heal the sick, what was he doing in retirement and in prayer?

His was the mission, not the power. Jesus said, " . . . the Son can do nothing by himself; he can do only what he sees the Father doing: and whatever the Father does the Son does too. For the Father loves the Son and shows him everything he does himself. . . "[16]

Jesus understood, above all, his need to return often to the Source of all he was. He withdrew to pray, not to escape his mission, but in order that he might fulfill it.

Often Jesus left the crowds, and even friends and family, to be alone to pray. The more involved he became with people, the greater his need for this seclusion.

The call to prayer is a call to rest, to solitude. When Jesus learned John the Baptist had been killed, he needed desperately to be alone. " . . . he withdrew by boat to a lonely place. . . "[17]

But the people followed him, seeking healing and, because of his compassion, Jesus stayed with them. Then he fed them fish and bread and sent them on their way, along with his disciples, for the need for solitude was still burning in his heart. " . . . he went up into the hills by himself to pray. When evening came, he was there alone, . . . "[18]

There, in the wilderness, where he could be nothing but himself, he came to know his poverty. There, in absolute aloneness, he knew he was with God.

He would leave the world behind, not for the ecstasy of communion, nor the security of his Father, but to see himself in the light of heaven, and to strip away what was not real.

He let himself be filled and nourished at his Father's table.

Jesus recognized the need of his friends to

take the time to rest and rejuvenate their souls also. "You must come away to some lonely place all by yourselves and rest for a while."[19]

So, also, must I leave the crowds and venture into the desert of prayer. No matter how busy I become, I must take the time my soul requires.

Do I not labor in the marketplace of life? Am I never burdened with the affairs of state?

"Come to me, all you who labor and are overburdened, and I will give you rest. Shoulder my yoke and learn from me, for I am gentle and humble in heart, and you will find rest for your souls. Yes, my yoke is easy and my burden light."[20]

Do I not lose contact with the Father in the crowd? Can I live without returning to the mountain's solitude?

But I need not really climb a mountain; I don't have to go away, for the One I seek in solitude, I will find within my soul.

In prayer, you make me lie down in green pastures, you lead me beside the still waters, you restore my soul.

VI

The Moment at Hand

I say I love you, God, but maybe I don't. I find myself spending so little time with you. Sometimes I realize I have not been with you for days. If love means presence, and if I love you, why am I not present to you?

I am like the disciples who came to the Garden of Gethsemani with Jesus. The Lord was sad and troubled. He needed to pray and he needed the presence of his friends. "My soul is sorrowful to the point of death. Wait here and keep awake with me."[21]

Even in prayer, Jesus was in agony. When he turned back to his disciples, he found them sleeping. "So you had not the strength to keep awake with me one hour? . . . You should be awake, and praying not to be put to the

test. The spirit is willing, but the flesh is weak."[22]

The first bird just sings out, Lord, declaring the day, even before I am ready for it. I see the dark of night turning purple-blue; soon the sun will have arisen too.

What will it be like today, Lord? Will it be the day I live abundantly, or will I just walk through the day without living? Will it be the day in which I remember you, or will the day's happenings be more important to me? Will it be the day that love rules, or will I look to self for everything? Will this be the last day of my life on earth, or will you give me yet another chance to know you?

And if I claim to know you in the morning, God, will I deny you at noon? Will I recognize you in the evening?

If I have nothing else, I have the moment at hand. Let me dedicate it to you, Father. Let me take my refreshment from your fountain.

Let me plan my day in such a way that prayer is the center, not an afterthought. You, my Father, are as important to me as the place you occupy in my daily schedule.

Let me wake each morning in an attitude of prayer. Let me remember you at noontime, and fall asleep with you at night. Let me fill the niches of my life with prayer.

Tomorrow's prayer begins today. At times, it might not come easily, but prayer is like mining for a precious metal. Much time and work is needed to separate and cast away the worthless ore for the sake of one ounce of treasure. That ounce will be my daily bread.

I have all eternity to pray, but let me remember that eternity is now.

VII

The Way of Totality

The way of prayer is the way of totality. There is no middle ground.

Jesus believed that through his interdependence with the Father, the kingdom of heaven had come. He dared not become autonomous and he asked the same of others.

"He who is not with me is against me, and he who does not gather with me scatters."[23]

To gather my total self in prayer I must integrate my mind, heart and body. To leave prayer only to the intellect, or senses, or emotion is to scatter and divide; for each faculty is apt to fight the other in an effort to dominate.

Experience has shown that I would rather do anything than occupy myself with God. My pretexts are legion.

My mind is preoccupied with the circumstances and conditions of my life. I am so anxious about what others say or think. Such thoughts fill me until there is no room for prayer. Even "good thoughts" crowd out the Spirit.

Hopes, ambitions and desires, even when they are considered good, can block the path of prayer. My heart is captured by emotion, and taken away from the quiet of God.

And so Jesus sounds a warning: "Watch yourselves, or your hearts will be coarsened with debauchery and drunkeness and the cares of life, . . . "[24]

My fear, my guilt, my feelings of uneasiness and frustration invade my soul, and still the impulse to pray. The sounds and sights of the world are like bells which call my attention away.

A great deal of my everyday life is possessed by something other than you, God. How I yearn for you. How little I have you, or you me.

My mind is like a whirlpool, spinning endlessly with thoughts and images and words. I don't even know what most of it means. I don't recognize the faces.

" 'What is your name?' Jesus asked. 'My name is legion,' he answered, 'for there are many of us.' "[25]

43

The static is like a trench between you and me, God, though I know it is not a permanent barrier. I must be faithful and patient. There is consolation in believing that even now, when I feel you are the farthest away from me, you are really the closest.

I try to think of you as I know I can, but my mind is filled with empty, silly, stupid thoughts that lead nowhere, except away from you.

Even in the work I do for you, Father, there is a danger. As my activity increases and I become more successful in what I am doing, I tend to trust my own plans, my own methods. Soon my prayers have diminished, and I begin to look solely to myself, forgetting you.

I am Martha who is busy about much serving, to whom Jesus says, "Martha, Martha . . . you worry and fret about so many things, and yet few are needed, indeed only one."[26]

I am called to be like Mary, seated at the feet of Jesus, of whom he says, she " . . . has chosen the better part; it is not to be taken from her."[27]

◆━◆━◆

I walked through the desert this morning. I know this only because at the end of my

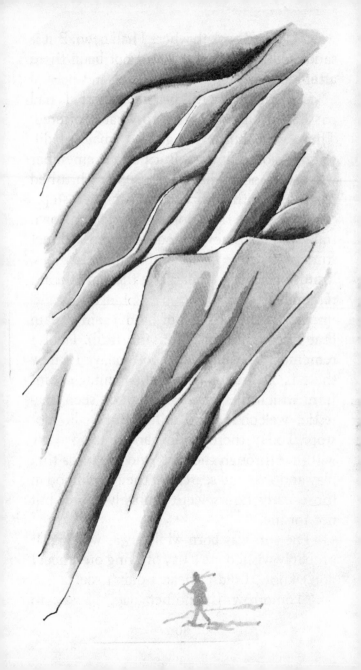

walk, I looked back to where I had been. But it saddened me to realize I had not been there after all.

Looking back, I saw the desert I had passed through, oblivious to what it offered. There were bushes, large and small, of different colored flowers. But I don't remember what they looked like, up close, for I brushed past them with a hurried, preoccupied step.

There were trails, interesting up and down trails. I only know I took the most direct route. If there were multicolored rocks, lizards or horned toads along the way, I don't remember.

I know there is a spot by the rain stream that smells different, pleasant, fresh. I don't remember passing that spot today. I know there is, at the top of a trail, a vantage point from which the mountains can be seen, majestic, welcoming, beautiful. But I did not stop. Today there is no panorama to carry with me through the day. And the birds that play and soar and search for their livelihood in those early hours were probably there, but not for me.

The sun was born while I was walking. It probably wished me a day of living presence. I don't know. I didn't hear. I didn't see.

"Tomorrow is another day," I say to

myself, attempting consolation. But that is the sad part ... tomorrow is another day. Today is gone forever.

⬖═══⬗

The antidote for distraction from prayer is prayer itself.

When my mind is filled with schemes for projects, world developments which overwhelm, or prideful thoughts which inflate my head, let me fast and pray.

"As for this kind, it is cast out only by prayer and fasting,"[28] Jesus told his disciples.

Let my mind be emptied of that which feeds its gluttonous machinery. Then let it fast until my Father comes to dine with me in prayer.

When ambition has me busy building towers into the sky, let me pray, meditating on death, and the vanity of it all.

When the happenings of yesterday bring depression and disgust; when tomorrow's possibilities choke today through fear and worry, let me pray and come to know the presence of the living God in whom there is no past, no future, only the I AM.

When the static of life makes me adverse to prayer, let me pray the more. When I find I

47

cannot pray as I would, let me pray as I can.

❖━━❖

Sweet, gentle Friend. How I abuse you and take you for granted. How I ignore you and step on you. And when I finally look your way, you smile at me and say, "Welcome back. It's all right. You are with me now."

Then, I look away and walk off into the darkness and the storm. But when I reach out for your hand again, you give me your peace.

"Peace I bequeath to you, my own peace I give you, a peace the world cannot give, this is my gift to you. Do not let your hearts be troubled or afraid."[29]

You are the glory of the universe, the center and cause of life itself, but in my heart you are second to trivia, to preoccupation, to fear and pride.

❖━━❖

Dear Friend. I love you so.
Dear Friend. I feel so loved.
Dear Friend. Take my hand,
take my mind and soul.
Dear Friend.

❖━━❖

VIII

My Heart Begins to Pray

Silence is the sound of my inmost prayer. Talking with my Father is prayer, to be sure. The spoken word brings focus to my intent; but when my mind runs out of thoughts and words, my heart begins to pray.

"In your prayers do not babble as the pagans do, for they think that by using many words they will make themselves heard. Do not be like them; your Father knows what you need before you ask him."[30]

I find words inadequate to communicate with you. It seems that words contain a desire to be heard or read. It is really only through love that I can be with you.

Silence is more than the absence of words. It leaves behind the clanging chains of thought and desire, habit and expectation.

The silence which I seek must come, not from the control of the external, but from the humble abandonment of the inner self.

My noisy life is like the man with an evil spirit who came into the synagogue screaming, "What do you want with us, Jesus of Nazareth? Have you come to destroy us? I know who you are: the Holy One of God."[31]

My silence in prayer is like the voice of Jesus saying, " 'Be quiet! Come out of him!' and the unclean spirit threw the man into convulsions and with a loud cry went out of him."[32]

Then my prayer abandons any purpose it might have had, seeking nothing but to rest in quiet faith and simple openness. The silence of my prayer transcends the noises of the world. The street sounds and the many voices do not disturb this peace. Instead, the stillness of the night drowns the clamor of the day.

He who is called to pray, let him listen.

The nature of prayer is a listening for the still, small voice of God. Only with the deepest silence of the heart can I hear your call, my Father, so fine, so subtle, so sublime. My prayer to you becomes a listening to your prayer in me.

❖━━❖

I went to my knees to pay homage to you; to be humble at your feet. There I met you on your knees too.

❖━━❖

I may expect to hear you in the thunder of the storm or the tolling of the bells, but your soothing voice is better heard in the small things near and dear to me.

I can hear you in the gentle breeze, the cricket, or in the laughter of a child. I can hear you in a sigh of love and the sweet song of a bird. I can hear you in the silent moments of my daily life.

My silent soul comes to you, Father, listening to your words: "Be still and know that I am God."[33]

IX

I Cease and You Become

The light of love makes me transparent. I cease and you become. This is my prayer's greatest attainment.

Through a death which comes in prayer, I am born anew. I discard the sense of knowing and doing, and enter spiritual childhood.

"So he called a little child to him and set the child in front of them. Then he said, 'I tell you solemnly, unless you change and become like little children you will never enter the kingdom of heaven.' "[34]

Yesterday I saw my little boy imitating my every move, my every gesture. He didn't know I was aware of him, he just wanted to be like me. I don't know if it was ego that made me feel a warm gratitude about it. I felt good that he loved me so much that he wanted to be like me.

As I reflect on it this morning, I wonder if this is how you feel when I love you enough to want to be like you, to imitate you, to be true to the way you made me in your image.

This self-abandonment comes when I abandon even the desire for self-abandonment and seek only to know you, Father.

I don't want to be the one who lives. Please, you take my place. You fill my soul, you live my moments. It must be you.

"This same joy I feel, and now it is complete. He must grow greater, I must grow smaller."[35]

I take pleasure in our encounter, but how I yearn for our communion. You are so good to me. Would that I loved you enough to exist only in you.

Give me the strength, the faith, the love that it takes to die. Give me the singlemindedness that lets me remember, "only one thing is necessary."

◈═══◈

Not to do, but to be.
Not to me, but through me.
Not for me, but from you.
Not to capture, but to abide.

◈═══◈

I begin to pass out of myself, empty myself, give myself. I find myself wanting nothing, asking for nothing, reaching for nothing. Not calling, but being called.

"If anyone wants to be a follower of mine, let him renounce himself and take up his cross and follow me. For anyone who wants to save his life will lose it; but anyone who loses his life for my sake, and for the sake of the gospel, will save it. What gain, then, is it for a man to win the whole world and ruin his life?"[36]

The kernel of myself is broken and its pieces dissolved in you, dear God.

As I deny myself in prayer I feel a sense of helplessness, frustration, infidelity, confusion, ignorance. I soon come to realize that I cannot pray by myself.

But my sense of sinfulness and indispensibility dies hard. Even as I realize that my prayer is not my own, but your prayer in me, I take the credit.

<hr />

I do not love you more than the dung of this world, much less do I love you more than my father, mother, wife and children. For above any love I may have for you, I love myself. Self is my ruler. No so much because self overpowers me, but because I abdicate

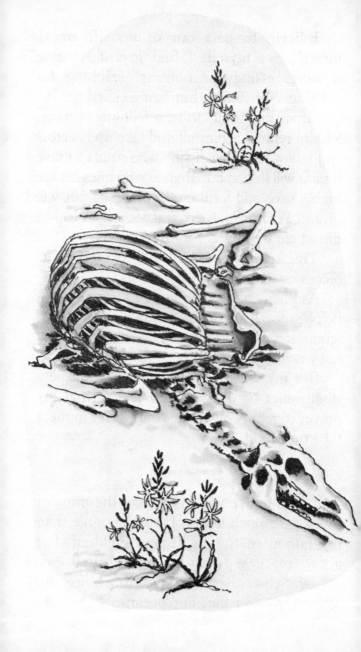

your reign to the kingdom of self, to the Prince of this world.

"Then leading him to a height, the devil showed him in a moment of time all the kingdoms of the world and said to him, 'I will give you all this power and the glory of these kingdoms, for it has been committed to me and I give it to anyone I choose. Worship me, then, and it shall all be yours.' But Jesus answered him, 'Scripture says: "You must worship the Lord your God, and serve him alone." ' "[37]

<hr/>

I cannot go with you, Evil One, though your call is sweet and alluring. I turn my head your way and death is so appealing. I know you have worked so hard to keep me busy and excited, but through the noise I hear the one small voice of he who loves me.

I cannot go with you, Evil One, who are so bright, so full of novelty and pleasure. I know I flirt with you and even lead you on. But through the clouds of tomorrow's fantasies, I can see the outstretched arms of he who loves me.

<hr/>

I am in a hurry to get to a place that doesn't exist. I am a battlefield.

My mind is so concentrated on myself that you become obscure. Help me disappear. Let your love overtake my soul.

"Having exhausted all these ways of tempting him, the devil left him, to return at the appointed time."[38]

Let go. Let go. I hear you calling to me. Empty. Empty.

Help me look beyond myself, beyond my helplessness and limitations, and to wait. As I lose my sense of self, I leave space and enter timelessness. I am praying, but I do not know it.

◈━━◈

I do not ask for understanding; I only ask for love. I do not ask for the world; I only ask for death. Let me die to self that I may have life.

◈━━◈

"I tell you, most solemnly, unless a wheat grain falls on the ground and dies, it remains only a simple grain; but if it dies, it yields a rich harvest. Anyone who loves his life loses it; anyone who hates his life in this world will keep it for the eternal life."[39]

X

Naked Before You

Where can I hide? In prayer my soul is naked before you.

Your eyes meet mine, and my heart must speak with candor.

If prayer is nothing else, it must be sincere.

"God is spirit, and those who worship must worship in spirit and truth."[40]

Many of my words are not real prayers because they do not represent my open spirit, and my most sincere surrender. Often, they are words I use to meet the expectations of others.

"And when you pray, do not imitate the hypocrites: they love to say their prayers standing up in the synagogues and at the street corners for people to see them. I tell you solemnly, they have their reward. But when you pray, go to your private room and, when you have shut your door, pray to your Father who is in that secret place, and your Father who sees all that is done in secret will reward you."[41]

The tie that binds me to you, Father, cannot by men be justified. For when I pray it is not duty, ritual or display. I meet you deep within, and here is where I stay; but the love that comes of union reaches out in every way.

My words and acts, however virtuous, are empty unless they come from love.

"If you remain in me and my words remain in you, you may ask what you will and you shall get it. It is to the glory of my Father that you should bear much fruit, and then you will be my disciples. As the Father has loved me, so I have loved you."[42]

Prayer is not always blissful, if it is honest, if it speaks truth and relates to life.

Knowing I cannot fool you, Father, with my pious sweet talk, knowing I must speak only the truth when I converse with you makes prayer painful for me. I find I cannot even call you "Dear" God because my life and my moment-by-moment thoughts show that in practice I do not hold you "dear" to me, at least not consciously.

To pray sincerely is to risk, for when I pray this way I do not know what will be asked of me.

Is this the fear of the Lord of which they speak? Well I do fear you, God. I fear the next step with you. You seem to want it all, and I seem to struggle to hold it back. It is as though I am willing to be in the same room with you, but I do not dare to look you in the eye, for then I could no longer lie. I could no longer hold fast to my life. I would have to die.

Jesus' promise that he who asks will receive, he who seeks will find, and to him who knocks the door will be opened can also be an admonition about prayer.

In the beginning, prayer is like the crowd which enthusiastically welcomed Jesus into the city. "Great crowds of people spread their cloaks on the road, while others were cutting branches from the trees and spreading them in his path. The crowds who went in front of him and those who followed were all shouting: 'Hosanna to the Son of David! Blessings on him who comes in the name of the Lord! Hosanna in the highest heavens.' "[43]

The initial ardor of prayer melts when it appears that it has been taken seriously. "And when he entered Jerusalem, the whole city was in turmoil. 'Who is this?' people asked, and the crowds answered, 'This is the prophet Jesus from Nazareth in Galilee.' "[44]

Then reality explodes. God has heard the prayer and has answered it. But am I ready for what his answer brings? "Jesus then went into the temple and drove out all those who were selling and buying there; he upset the tables of the money changers and the chairs of those who were selling pigeons."[45]

Prayer is a serious business.

If my prayer asks for health and happiness for myself and others, your answer may require that I cast away a hurtful habit to which I cling with fear. It may demand that I do your bidding and represent your love.

When I ask sincerely that the poor be helped, it may be that the help can only come from me.

If I pray for humility, I will be taken at my word. I may not be considered saintly. Instead, I may be ridiculed, misunderstood and rejected by the world.

I pray to be like Jesus. Am I sincere?

<hr>

How lonely you were — I have many friends.
How hated you were — I am loved.

How hungry you were — I am
    satisfied.
How poor you were — I have no
    needs unmet.
How much pain you felt — I do
    not hurt.
How well you know me — I know you
    not.

❖━━━❖

I pray the words of Jesus. Am I sincere or is this closer to the truth:

Our Father (most of the time I call you "my" Father or I do not call you at all), who art in heaven (generally, I am not aware of where you are and, usually, I don't care), hallowed be your name (it is my name that is hallowed in my day-to-day life, not yours).

Your kingdom come (I may pay lip service to that, but the reality is that I shudder to imagine what it would really mean if your kingdom were to come. It would mean the end of my kingdom), your will be done (I can say it, but my life shows I really don't desire it) on earth as it is in heaven (as long as I'm in control of earth, it will not be as it is in heaven).

Give us this day our daily bread (Mostly I just take what I need, and when I run out, I cry for more. When there is plenty it is because I provide it. When there is scarcity it is because you are holding back), and forgive us our trespasses as we forgive those who trespass against us (No! Wait! Forgive me my trespasses, but don't tie it to my forgiving others or I will never be forgiven).

Lead us not into temptation (Yes, give me the strength to resist temptation — but not just yet), but deliver us from evil (Let me do what I want, how I want, and you cover me) for yours is the kingdom and the power and the glory forever and ever (next to mine). Amen.

The truth is:

We love you as much as we love one another. We accept your forgiveness as we accept it of ourselves.

We are as merciful as we are open to your mercy.

Our faith takes us as far as our eyes can see and our ears can hear.

Our hope is tied to what we earn and deserve.

You are as alive in us as the things of the world are dead.

You are here and now as much as we are here and now.

You are our Father as much as we are

64

your children.

I feel as though I knock on your door and run away before you answer. When you open the door to let me in, I am down the street looking for you where you are not.

Sometimes I come close to despair. I forget where the door is. Then, through your gentle nudge, you remind me. Yet I hesitate to knock for fear the door will open, just as you say. Then I will be invited in empty-handed. Can I risk empty-handedness? Dare I forsake all for the other side?

A certain man asked Jesus what he must do to have eternal life. When Jesus offered him life through obedience to God's commandments the man replied, " 'I have kept all these. What more do I need to do?' Jesus said, 'If you wish to be perfect, go and sell what you own and give the money to the poor, and you will have treasure in heaven; then come, follow me.' But when the young man heard these words he went away sad, for he was a man of great wealth."[46]

I too go away sad, rejecting Jesus' way. The possessions he asks me to abandon are not material, but they weigh me down. They have little value, but I've sold my soul for them.

Lord, if you are with me where is my scandal?

Lord, if you live in me where is my suffering?

Lord, if you love through me where is my flower?

Lord, my pasture is green, my bins are full, my children are safe in bed.

Where are the boards, the nails and the thorns?

Where is the scourging, the spittle, the scorn?

Where is the night?

My Lord, my Lord. Why have I forsaken you?

◆━━◆

My prayer, if it is sincere, summons from my depths a full and personal response to life.

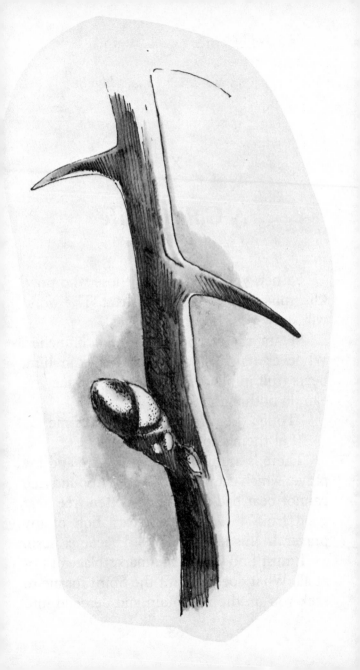

XI

A Call to Life

Father, you live through those who pray. Our mission is to bear your fruit. The world will know you through our lives.

"I am the vine, you are the branches. Whoever remains in me, with me in him, bears fruit in plenty; for cut off from me you can do nothing."[47]

"Touch them for me," you ask of me.

"Let them know I love them."

There is a unity between my life and my prayer which cannot be denied. "A sound tree cannot bear bad fruit, nor a rotten tree bear good fruit."[48] I am the incarnation of my prayer. In this sense, the Word becomes flesh.

I must find you in the marketplace or not at all. What does it profit the Spirit for me to seek you on the mountain and descend into the valley without you?

Jesus took his disciples and went up the mountain to pray. On the mountain these men saw and heard the spirit of God and told Jesus, "Master, it is wonderful for us to be here. . . ."[49] They were content with their Lord alone on the mountain. Yet, on the next day, Jesus brought them down from the mountain into a waiting crowd of people with many needs.

I may share a quiet moment with you, Father, in the secret closet of my soul, but you do not let me stay for long. You send me out that I may share in public what you have shared with me in private.

Today I give myself to you that you may love others through me, and that they may love you through me. Let my life be your uttered word.

"I give you a new commandment: love one another; just as I have loved you, you also must love one another. By this love you have for one another, everyone will know that you are my disciples."[50]

<hr/>

Sometimes, in my exuberance, I deliver myself to you even unto death. As when Peter said to Jesus, "Why can't I follow you now? I will lay down my life for you."[51]

Then the hard part comes. I am asked, not to die for you, but to live, really live. But it is easier to die, and so much more exciting, so much more praiseworthy, so much more finished.

My salvation is that you will not let me die until I have lived, until I have known you.

I will stay with you forever!
"Stay with me this moment."
I will die for you!
"Live for me."
I will sacrifice for you!
"Only love me."
Hear my prayer!
"I cannot hear you in prayer if I cannot
hear you in life."

To pray is, above all, to be human and to identify myself with all of humanity. There can be no prayer in isolation from the world.

"Then the king will say to those on his right hand, 'Come, you whom my Father has blessed, take for your heritage the kingdom prepared for you since the foundation of the world. For I was hungry and you gave me

food; I was thirsty and you gave me drink; I was a stranger and you made me welcome; naked and you clothed me, sick and you visited me, in prison and you came to see me.'

"Then the virtuous will say to him in reply, 'Lord, when did we see you hungry and feed you; or thirsty and give you drink? When did we see you a stranger and make you welcome; naked and clothe you; sick or in prison and go to see you?' And the King will answer, 'I tell you solemnly, in so far as you did this to one of the least of these brothers of mine, you did it to me.' "[52]

My life reflects the nature of my prayers. If I would love you, Father, in spirit, then I will love your children. If I am open, present and honest with you in prayer, then I will be so with others.

❖━━❖

Who am I living for? Now is the time to know.

If I love you, why am I sacrificing lambs instead of feeding your sheep?

Let me recognize you in my brother, and love you therein.

The faces fade, the shadows grow into each other. "You are" becomes "I am."

72

There are voices, lonely, helpless, searching for their home. I must soothe them. I must tell them that there is peace within.

The end of this journey is near, and the death which overtakes is life itself.

In prayer I awaken to the presence and the needs of others. In prayer is the fountain of my brotherhood. In prayer is the treasure of the kingdom.

I want to be a good father.
"Then learn to be my son."

I want to be a good husband.
"Then marry me."

I want to be a good friend.
"Then die for me."

I want to be a good worker.
"Then take my yoke."

I want to be holy.
"Then don't want it."

I want to love you.
"Then accept my love for you."

"When a man has had a great deal given him, a great deal will be demanded of him; when a man has had a great deal given him on trust, even more will be expected of him."[53]

———

Then I will accomplish much!
"Accomplish nothing, but live fully."
You are my Ruler!
"I am your Lover."
I will give you what I have!
"Be little and powerless."

———

Love is nothing if it is not everything. Without love, I live. With love, you live through me.

Through life you call me to prayer, and through prayer you call me back to life.

XII

Your Will Becomes My Own

Jesus' disciples disbelieved their eyes when a fig tree withered at their Master's command. They too, he told them, could wither a fig tree, move a mountain or receive all things for which they asked in prayer and in faith.

Does this mean, then, that I too can have what I will if only I pray for it with sufficient faith and perseverence? I doubt that is what Jesus' words to his companions meant.

Rather, the disciples were being called by their Master to pray, not so that their wills would be realized, but that the will of their Father in heaven would be done.

Jesus knew that when I pray in loving, open faith, my will fades like a shadow and I find myself asking for your will, my Father. As

75

I seek your will, I let it be done.

Too often I view prayer as an attempt to enlighten you, God, as to what is needed, then to coax you, bribe you, and beg you to meet that need. But prayer does not make of you a mere means to serve some selfish and external end of mine. Nor does it use you as some kind of superman on whom I call to protect me in case of danger.

The root of my frustration is the unfulfillment of my own plans.

The way toward peace is to discard my plans, and wait for the reality you give me.

It is so easy for me to talk to you, but so hard for me to talk with you. It is easy for me to make petitions of you, but difficult to listen to your petitions of me.

Jesus knew his need for you was greater than his earthly needs. He asked those who would hear him to transcend their temporal needs and seek, instead, to satisfy their greatest need of all.

"That is why I am telling you not to worry about your life and what you are to eat, nor about your body and how you are to clothe it."[54]

"Set your hearts on his kingdom first, and on his righteousness, and all these other things will be given you as well."[55]

If the needs I want met cause me to turn to you, Father, let me be grateful that they lead me to the field. But then, when I find the treasure in the field, let my needs be cast away.

"It is too small and unsatisfactory, whatsoever you bestow on me apart from yourself."[56]

To know this need for you, my Father, makes me your child. "How happy are the poor in spirit; theirs is the kingdom of heaven."[57]

To enter the kingdom into which I am invited, let my prayer be an asking, a seeking and a knocking at the door of my heart.

"Ask, and it will be given to you; search, and you will find; knock, and the door will be opened to you. For the one who asks always receives; the one who searches always finds; the one who knocks will always have the door opened to him."[58]

But it is not enough to speak your name or to praise you with my words. Through love I let you live in me, and your will becomes my own.

"It is not those who say to me, 'Lord, Lord,' who will enter the kingdom of heaven, but the person who does the will of my Father in heaven."[59]

Therefore, when I pray, intent upon your will, Father, the power of eternal love explodes into my life.

◈═══◈

Not what do I do Lord, but who does it through me.

Not where do I go Lord, but who goes there with me.

Not who am I Lord, but who we are.

◈═══◈

Through prayer I place myself at your disposal. "Your will be done on earth (in my life) as it is in heaven (in my heart)."

Your sweet and gentle ways meet my hardness, and give life to my core. From you, I gather strength and purpose. To you who are eternal and present, I return just as I came.

Who I am, Dear Love, is in your hands. You know that I want to die to self, and let you live in me. I see now that even this is under your control, not mine. I find I must let go even of my effort to be holy, and only look to you.

Through prayer I become the arms with which you embrace the world. Through me, you offer peace and harmony to those who

78

live around me.

Through prayer I come to know your will and, through prayer, I receive the strength to carry it out.

❖━━❖

I do want to die, God, but I am afraid of what it will really mean. I am afraid that it will not be the saintly life of which I read in books, but rather a life of the cross to which you show the way. I refuse. I don't want it. I love my squalor, my blindness, my world.

Dear God, if it be your will that I die to this world and take up your yoke, in order to live a more abundant life, then let it be done.

❖━━❖

From the Center comes the light which chases the shadows from my path.

I feel a sense of peace. I want to grow where I have been planted. I feel like settling down to business, like taking a risk and living. I feel like committing myself, like letting go, letting it happen — in spite of myself. I don't know what you want to do with me tomorrow, but I do know what you want to do with me this moment. Somehow, this is enough for me to know.

Let me accept my cup of life as Jesus accepted his cup of death. " 'My Father,' he said, 'if it is possible, let this cup pass me by. Nevertheless, let it be as you, not I, would have it.' "[60]

XIII

Single Eye

Prayer is the centering of all that I am in absorbed attention on you, my heavenly Father.

❦

You don't want me to "be good,"
you want me to love you.

You don't want me to live rightly,
you want me to live completely.

You don't want me to know about
you, you want me to know you.

❦

Prayer is not a focusing on something outside myself, but a turning within to a profound consciousness of your presence.

You want all of me, not just the few
morsels of myself which I steal from the world

and smuggle to you in the darkness.

How can I love you? By letting you love me.

Even as a baby there was no room for him. The world was crowded, the rooms filled. Would that I could change that now; that he might find room in my soul to reside forever. Would that my heart was not crowded with the world. Only singleness of mind and spirit can reserve for you the whole house.

Jesus was ever conscious of you, Father. This consciousness was the kingdom of heaven to which he constantly compared the valuables of the world.

"The kingdom of heaven is like treasure hidden in a field which someone has found; he hides it again, goes off happy, sells everything he owns and buys the field."[61]

◆━━◆━━◆

I have been placed in the eye of the hurricane and I feel destruction when I leave it.

You have asked of me the Oneness of One. I am only a part, and life comes only to the whole.

You are my Father. You are my Brother. You are me.

Your presence in my life is the kingdom of heaven. I cherish it more than life itself. I will pay the price to know it forever.

But the cost of such a consciousness is high. To pay it, I must sell all that I possess.

I must sell my memories of years gone by, and my future plans for a moment in your presence now. I must sell the high esteem in which I would be held, and the goods I have acquired, for humility and poverty before you. I must sell my wise and prudent thoughts and the pleasure of my senses for one measure of your love for me.

I must relinquish my own will, for the death and resurrection of my soul.

Stripped of my possessions, I have only to attend to you.

I can give you only what I own. If I have nothing, I can give you my soul.

You, only, shall I love with all my heart. "I ask nothing of You. I do not ask even your love. I want only You."[62]

Help me to love you so, Dear God, that I would give up heaven, that I would pass up a look at your face, that I would enter hell for you.

You only shall I hold in thought. " . . . she, the faithful one whose mind is steadfast, who keeps the peace because she trusts in you."[63]

You, only, shall I see. "The lamp of your body is your eye. When your eye is sound, your whole body too is filled with light. . . ."[64]

XIV

Through the Cloud of Separation

The skies were dark and the world had turned against him.

His muscles quivered with pain, nails pierced his flesh, and thorns dug deep into his scalp. Would anyone help him? Why was he so alone? "My God, my God, why have you deserted me?"[65]

He had known well the presence of his Father in his life, even through the horror of that night. But there was a time, on that tree of torture, when he felt abandoned, even by his God.

Yet from the abyss of nothingness, and through the cloud of separation, came the cry of faithful death, "Father, into your hands I commit my spirit."[66]

I who have known your presence, Father,

have also known my absence from you. These times of perdition come like a thief in the night, and strip me of the joy I thought forever mine.

And try as I might, I cannot regain your presence through my own efforts. This state of separation is not my true nature and turns into a living hell. "My heart within is desolate."

It is a dark night. Seeds seem to fall on shallow ground. I am closed to you. There has not been love. I was too close to you and it frightened me. I fled to the comfort of ignorance.

Life appears complicated. I am reacting to it impulsively, without love to guide me. I am a captive, and it appears that I love my jailer more than freedom.

❦❦❦

I am divided. I am segregated.
I am out of focus.
I am running fast. I am anxious.

❦❦❦

Whether or not it was you I saw today, Jesus, it was you.

Your apparel was sackcloth, with a white robe-like garment underneath. Your hair was dark brown and long, much as we see in paintings of you.

It was drizzling and you were a little wet. Your bare feet walked along South Park Avenue. You were looking at the ground as you moved. You were sad, it seemed.

When I first saw you, my heart skipped several beats and I just stared, not believing my eyes.

As I drove on, I looked through the rearview mirror, and you had not stopped. You walked as though you had a destination.

I kept driving, switching my thoughts to my destination. Then it hit me. You and I were travelling in opposite directions.

My soul is in transition. I experience dark, dark times of faithlessness and deadness. I know I hurt those I love in the name of efficiency and pride and by my spiritual absence from them.

I find myself at the bottom of a dark, empty hole and I cannot see the light at the top. Then by a faith that comes, not from my doubting heart, but as a gift from you who love me, even through the cloud of separation, I am reaching up, hoping, yes, believing that you will clench my desperate hand and

pull me out of the abyss slowly, allowing me to use my own footing as I climb out into the light.

To despair is to be attached to the consequences of my life. To hope is to rely on those circumstances with which I have nothing to do. It is from this poverty of soul that I must pray, believing.

◆━━◆━━◆

When the feeling of hope is dead, expect.
When the consolation of faith has left,
    believe.
When the joy of charity is gone, love.

◆━━◆━━◆

In defiance of all apparent evidence, and contrary to what I feel within, I believe that you are near me, and I accept your constant love.

Like the melting snow, my hardness falls away. Through loosened soil, my life comes back to me. What is this Spring that waited for its time, that loved me even through the winter cold? The fruit it brings was once a dying seed, a patient, pregnant Source of all there is.

My Lord, my Lord. What ecstasy! You are with me. You are all around me, everywhere I turn, in every face, in every rock, in all there is and in all who are.

My heart is pregnant with *agape*. I am even afraid to hear your word lest I explode. I love you so this moment. I feel your love for me so loudly and clearly through our world and all who are a part of it. We are one, you and us. Can heaven be more than this?

So warm, so gentle, so full of love, yet I will go away.

You are my life, you are my purpose, you are my soul, yet I will go away.

If only I would stay a while longer, if only I would pray just one more time, if only I would touch your hand before I fall away.

If I would share your warmth and gentleness, if I would pass the cup of love, if I would spark the lives of others and give them hope and light, then I would stay a while longer, I would feel your sweet caress. I would stay a while longer, or I may not leave at all.

Citations

1. Mark 1:35
2. Matthew 22:37-38
3. Matthew 22:39-40
4. Luke 1:30-32
5. John 1:23
6. Matthew 5:23-25
7. John 1:4
8. John 3:8
9. Matthew 11:25-26
10. John 3:3
11. Matthew 23:25
12. Luke 11:1
13. Matthew 6:9-13
14. Mark 12:44
15. Luke 5:15-16
16. John 5:19-20
17. Matthew 14:13

18. Matthew 14:23-24
19. Mark 6:31
20. Matthew 11:28-30
21. Matthew 26:38-39
22. Matthew 26:40-42
23. Matthew 12:30-31
24. Luke 21:34
25. Mark 5:9-10
26. Luke 10:41-42
27. Luke 10:42
28. Matthew 17:21
29. John 14:27
30. Matthew 6:7-9
31. Mark 1:24-25
32. Mark 1:26-27
33. Psalm 46:10
34. Matthew 18:2-3
35. John 3:29-30
36. Mark 8:34-37
37. Luke 4:5-8
38. Luke 4:13
39. John 12:24-25
40. John 4:24
41. Matthew 6:5-6
42. John 15:7-9
43. Matthew 21:8-9
44. Matthew 21:10-11
45. Matthew 21:12-13
46. Matthew 19:20-22

BREAD FOR THE EATING $1.95

Kelly B. Kelly. Sequel to the popular **Grains of Wheat,** this book of words received in prayer draws the reader closer to God through imagery. Excellent meditation aid.

GRAINS OF WHEAT $1.95

Kelly B. Kelly. This little book of words received in prayer is filled with simple yet often profound leadings, exhortations and encouragement for daily living. By the author of **Bread for the Eating.**

THE BORN-AGAIN CATHOLIC $3.50

Albert H. Boudreau. This book presents an authoritative imprimatur treatment of today's most interesting religious issue. The author, a Catholic layman, looks at Church tradition past and present and shows that the born-again experience is not only valid, but actually is Catholic Christianity at its best. The exciting experience is not only investigated, but the reader is guided into revitalizing his or her own Christian experience. The informal style, colorful personal experiences, and helpful diagrams make this book enjoyable and profitable reading.

THE BOOK OF REVELATION: What Does It Really Say? $1.95

Rev. John Randall, S.T.D. The most discussed book of the Bible today is examined by a scripture expert in relation to much that has been published on the Truth. A simply written and revealing presentation.

LINGER WITH ME
Moments Aside With Jesus $2.95

Rev. Msgr. David E. Rosage. God is calling us to a listening posture in prayer in the desire to experience him at the very core of our being. Monsignor Rosage helps us to "come by ourselves apart" daily and listen to what Jesus is telling us in Scripture.

PRAYING WITH MARY $2.50

Msgr. David E. Rosage. This book is one avenue which will help us discover ways and means to satisfy our longing for prayer and a more personal knowledge of God. Prayer was Mary's life-style. As we come to know more about her life of prayer we will find ourselves imitating her in our approach to God.

UNION WITH THE LORD IN PRAYER
Beyond Meditation to Affective Prayer
Aspiration and Contemplation $1.00

Venard Polusney, O. Carm. "A magnificent piece of work. It touches on all the essential points of Contemplative Prayer. Yet it brings such a sublime subject down to the level of comprehension of the 'man in the street,' and in such an encouraging way."
Abbott James Fox, O.C.S.O. (former superior of Thomas Merton at the Abbey of Gethsemane).

A DESERT PLACE